Curriculum Vision

Spelling

Teacher's Resource Book

2

Sarah Lindsay

Curriculum Visions

Spelling

First published in 2006 by
Atlantic Europe Publishing Company Ltd

Text copyright © Sarah Lindsay and
Richard Jackman 2006

The right of Sarah Lindsay and Richard Jackman
to be identified as the authors of this work have
been asserted by them in accordance with the
Copyright, Designs and Patents Act 1988.

Illustrations and design copyright © 2006
Atlantic Europe Publishing Company Ltd

Curriculum Visions Spelling
Teacher's Resource Book 2
A CIP record for this book is available
from the British Library.

ISBN-10: 1-86214-517-2
ISBN-13: 978-1-86214-517-7

**This product is manufactured from sustainable
managed forests. For every tree cut down at least
one more is planted.**

Author
Sarah Lindsay

Art Director
Duncan McCrae

Senior Designer
Adele Humphries

Editors
Robert Anderson and Gillian Gatehouse

Illustrations
Dave Woodroffe

Designed and produced by
EARTHSCAPE EDITIONS

Printed in China by
WKT Company Ltd

Contents

An Introduction to *Curriculum Visions Spelling*

Why should we teach spelling?

Effective spelling is central to a child's self-confidence. Being able to spell competently means confident writing. This is a motivating factor in the learning and enjoyment of all writing tasks across the curriculum, and in having the confidence to become better spellers. So, teaching the basic foundations for good spelling can trigger a virtuous cycle.

Spelling competence is also perceived within society as indicative of a level of literacy, educational attainment and intellect. Critically, a competent speller is less likely to be judged negatively in these respects as he or she moves through schooling and eventually into further education and employment.

Despite this, national test results continue to suggest that overall there is still an inadequate knowledge among some pupils of spelling rules and conventions. However, an organised and systematic approach to the teaching of spelling, as contained within the heart of the National Literacy Strategy, has been shown to raise levels of achievement significantly in those schools making a real commitment to the improvement of spelling.

The NLS

The NLS Framework for Teaching posits that pupils become successful readers by learning to use a range of strategies to get to the meaning of a text: phonic; grammatical knowledge; word recognition and graphic knowledge; context cues. It states that although teachers know about these strategies they are often 'over cautious about the teaching of phonics – sound and spelling'. It says that:

It is vital that pupils are taught to use these word level strategies effectively. Research evidence shows that pupils do not learn to distinguish between the different sounds of words simply by being exposed to books.

They need to be taught to do this. When they begin to read, most pupils tend to see words as images with a particular shape and pattern. They tend not to understand that words are made up of letters used in particular combinations that correspond with spoken sounds. It is essential that pupils are taught these basic decoding and spelling skills from the outset.

(NLS Framework for Teaching, page 4)

Curriculum Visions Spelling – An effective word level strategy

The Framework makes it clear that there should be a 'strong and systematic emphasis' on the teaching of spelling. So how does *Curriculum Visions Spelling* support the objectives of the Framework? The word level skill objectives in the NLS Framework include:

▶ the ability to discriminate between the separate sounds in words;

▶ the learning of the letters and letter combinations most commonly used to spell these sounds;

▶ the ability to write words by combining the spelling patterns of their sounds.

Curriculum Visions Spelling is absolutely focused on meeting these objectives, and does so in a clear, easy-to-follow and systematic fashion. It maps closely to the spelling and vocabulary objectives of the word level strand in the Framework at Key Stages 1 and 2 and helps you, the teacher, achieve both balance and coverage of the spelling-related objectives specified for each term.

Curriculum Visions Spelling also complements programmes based on synthetic phonics.

Word Level
Reception year
• Phonological awareness, phonics and spelling
• Word recognition, graphic knowledge and spelling
• Vocabulary extension
Key Stage 1
• Phonological awareness, phonics and spelling
• Word recognition, graphic knowledge and spelling
• Vocabulary extension
Key Stage 2
• Revision and consolidation from Key Stage 1 (to the end of Y3)
• Spelling strategies
• Spelling conventions and rules
• Vocabulary extension

How does *Curriculum Visions Spelling* deliver an effective spelling programme?

Curriculum Visions Spelling is designed to be easy for you to use by being structured in a way that children will find accessible, with clear targets and differentiated tasks.

The instructional language is clear, direct and carefully tailored to the needs of pupils at each level and age group. The activities are gently differentiated in difficulty and will help build pupils' confidence and reinforce their spelling knowledge, skills and competence.

We have thought long and hard about the layout and content of each unit. Our intention has been to provide you, the teacher, with a progressive and useful scheme for delivering the word level work in the NLS. The scheme has also been structured and devised to accommodate the requirements of teachers delivering the curricula of Scotland, Wales and Northern Ireland.

The main features of both the *Pupil Book* and *Teacher's Resource Book* are shown below.

Pupil Book

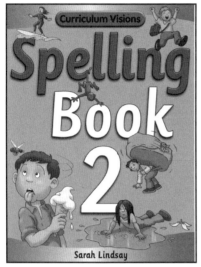

You will find me throughout the units. I am used to lighten the content for the child whilst also acting as a teaching tool! I remind the children of previously covered themes or teaching points.

Spelling focus

Each unit has a particular spelling as its main focus. The labelled picture helps the child recognise the focus of the unit immediately.

Word list

There follows four columns of words that relate to the *Spelling focus* of the unit. The *Word list* is intended as an aid to children working through the unit, particularly in the *Finding words* section. These words, where possible, increase in difficulty. They can be found listed in the *Look Cover Say Write Check* photocopiable tables (pages 87–93 of this book), ideal to be used as daily/weekly spellings. You, as the teacher, will need to decide which child should receive which spelling lists – one particular child might be given the first column to learn whilst the next child is challenged with the first three columns to learn.

Finding words

This is a gentle introduction to the words within the unit *Spelling focus*. It encourages the children to make words with related spellings.

Using words

This section extends the child's knowledge of the *Spelling focus*. He or she will have to search beyond the words found in the *Word list* for answers.

Puzzle corner

The *Puzzle corner* is a more light-hearted exercise that often focuses on vocabulary work. Where possible it is linked to the *Spelling focus* of the unit.

Teacher's Resource Book

Targets

These are the targets specifically covered in this unit, both in the *Spelling focus* and the *Puzzle corner* exercise.

Word list

A quick reference for the teacher. It is particularly useful when planning either different group work or spelling homework for individual children.

Some other relevant words

This list covers further words using the spelling patterns found in the *Word list*. In addition, other words are provided that might be useful for extension work or classroom discussions.

Pupil Book answers

These are the answers to the *Pupil Book* material.

Copymaster/ Homework answers

These are the answers to the photocopiable pages that link with the *Spelling focus* (Copymaster A) and the activity encompassed within the *Puzzle corner* (Copymaster B) of each unit. The work covered in the unit is reinforced and sometimes taken on a step further. Both activity sheets are ideal as homework or as further work in the classroom.

Relevant high-frequency words

High-frequency words that can be linked to the spelling focus of the unit.

Suggestions

A few extension activities have been suggested and/or background information provided.

Assessments

There are two assessments found on pages 82–83 and 84–85, each one covering either the first 11 units or the second 11 units. Notes and Answers to the Assessments can be found on page 81.

Word lists

The *Word lists* (copies of the *Word list* found in each unit) on pages 88–93 are designed to be photocopied and used as the spelling homework for the week. If required they can be used in conjunction with the *Look Cover Say Write Check* table found on page 96. The words can be split according to the ability of the child.

There are then further *Word lists* on pages 93–95 that cover (in groups of six words) the high-frequency words with which the children should become familiar as quickly as possible.

Scheme summary

	Book 1		Book 2		Book 3	
Unit 1	a	alphabetical order	ea ee	plurals (+s)	a–e ai ay	verb + ing
Unit 2	e	equipment labels	ay a–e ai	vowel / consonant	ee ea	syllables
Unit 3	i	high-frequency words	y i–e igh	common irregular words	ie i–e y igh	misspelt words
Unit 4	o	common spelling patterns	o–e oa ow	past tense (+ed)	o–e oa ow	categorising words
Unit 5	u	alphabetical order	ew ue u–e oo	high-frequency words	oo ew u–e ue	inferring meaning
Unit 6	sh	words within words	ck	present tense (+ing)	le	synonyms
Unit 7	ch	colour words	u oo	collections of words	un dis	thesaurus work
Unit 8	th	topic words	ar	antonyms	air are ear ere	dictionary work
Unit 9	ll	high-frequency words	oy oi	high-frequency words	or ore aw au	root words
Unit 10	ss ff	classroom captions	ow ou	syllables	er ir ur	dialogue words
Unit 11	ng	days of the week	tch nch	same sound, different spelling pattern	de re pre	opposites
Unit 12	cl fl sl	words within words	air	un prefix	+ y	compound words
Unit 13	dr gr tr	plurals (+s)	are ear	compound words	+ er + est	singular and plural
Unit 14	nd	word collections	or ore	dis prefix	n't	definitions
Unit 15	st sp	high-frequency words	aw au	syllables	silent k and w	verb + ing
Unit 16	str	ed endings	er	synonyms	+ ly	alphabetical order (second place)
Unit 17	nk	vowel letters	ir	same spelling pattern, different sound	+ ful + less	inferring meaning
Unit 18	ee	months of the year	ur	common irregular words	plurals	homonyms
Unit 19	ai	common spelling patterns	wh ph ch	ful suffix	mis	short words in longer words
Unit 20	ie i–e	consonant letters	wa	high-frequency words	qu	expressions
Unit 21	oa	ing endings	ear	ly suffix	apostrophe	synonyms
Unit 22	oo	numbers to twenty	ea	shades of meaning	non ex anti	dictionary work

	Book 4		Book 5		Book 6	
Unit 1	less ness	misspelt words	ch	plurals (es)	soft c and g	connectives
Unit 2	er	homophones	ent ence	misspelt words	silent letters	misspelt words
Unit 3	al	definitions	ant ance	expressions	able ible	unstressed vowels
Unit 4	ment	high-frequency words	auto bi	words ending in a, i, o and u	aero auto aqua	spelling similar words
Unit 5	verb + s ed ing	irregular tense changes	ly	plurals (ies)	bi con co	words changing over time
Unit 6	hood ship	alphabetical order (third place)	tele trans circum	synonyms	graph scope	origins of proper names
Unit 7	on en	making verbs	words to watch	plurals (ves)	cc	new words
Unit 8	double letters	changing vocabulary	silent letters b g c	onomatopoeia	tele tri oct	etymological dictionary
Unit 9	ic	alternative words	ful	double consonants (+ ed + ing)	dge age	mnemonics
Unit 10	un re non dis	gender words	letter strings	technical words	gue	unstressed vowels
Unit 11	words ending in f	definitions	soft c	antonyms	ex sub	word origins
Unit 12	ight	alphabetical order (fourth place)	soft g	homophones	ic	proverbs
Unit 13	ory ery ary	making adjectives	ure	possessive pronouns	ous	words changing over time
Unit 14	ough	medium-frequency words	al	expressions	inter micro	argument words
Unit 15	able	compound words	el	acronyms	dd	spelling rules
Unit 16	ible	diminutives	un im il	omission of letters	ist ian	mnemonics
Unit 17	ive	prefixes	er est ish	personally written definitions	or ar	misspelt words
Unit 18	ie ei	misspelt words	ion	thesaurus work	ary ery ory	dictionary work
Unit 19	tion	its and it's	en ify ise	modifying e	words to watch	spelling rules
Unit 20	sion	homophones	tt	changing tenses	nn	similes and metaphors
Unit 21	wa	suffixes	aw au	unstressed vowels	ise	word games
Unit 22	ss	root words	ph	dialect variations	ive	inventing words

Book 2 targets

Unit page	Spelling focus	Targets	Puzzle corner	Targets
Unit 1	ea ee	• to secure identification, spelling and reading of long vowel digraphs *ea ee* in simple words • to revise and extend the reading and spelling of words containing different spellings of the long vowel phoneme *ee*	plurals (+s)	• to use word ending *s* (plural) to support reading and spelling.
Unit 2	ay a–e ai	• to secure identification, spelling and reading of long vowel digraphs *ay a–e ai* in simple words • to revise and extend the reading and spelling of words containing different spellings of the long vowel phoneme *ai*	vowel/ consonant	• to secure understanding and use of the terms 'vowel' and 'consonant'
Unit 3	y i-e igh	• to secure identification, spelling and reading of long vowel digraphs *y i–e igh* in simple words • to revise and extend the reading and spelling of words containing different spellings of the long vowel phoneme *ie*	common irregular words	• to spell selected common irregular words
Unit 4	o–e oa ow	• to secure identification, spelling and reading of long vowel digraphs *o–e oa ow* in simple words • to revise and extend the reading and spelling of words containing different spellings of the long vowel phoneme *oa*	past tense (+ed)	• to use the word ending *ed* (past tense) to support reading and spelling
Unit 5	ew ue u–e oo	• to secure identification, spelling and reading of long vowel digraphs *ew ue u–e oo* in simple words • to revise and extend the reading and spelling of words containing different spellings of the long vowel phoneme *oo*	high- frequency words	• to read on sight and spell selected high-frequency words.
Unit 6	ck	• to secure the spelling of words ending in *ck*	present tense (+ing)	• to use the word ending *ing* to support reading and spelling.
Unit 7	u oo	• to recognise the common spelling patterns for the vowel phoneme *oo* • to identify the phonemes in speech and writing • to segment the words into phonemes for spelling • to investigate and classify words with the same sounds but different spellings	collections of words	• to learn to spell significant words of personal interest

Spelling Book 2 • Book 2 targets • © *Sarah Lindsay/Atlantic Europe Publishing 2006*

Unit page	Spelling focus	Targets	Puzzle corner	Targets
Unit 8	ar	• to recognise the common spelling patterns for the vowel phoneme *ar* • to identify the phonemes in speech and writing • to segment the words into phonemes for spelling • to investigate and classify words with the same sounds but different spellings	antonyms	• to introduce the use of antonyms: collect, discuss differences of meaning and their spelling
Unit 9	oy oi	• to recognise the common spelling patterns for the vowel phoneme *oy* • to identify the phonemes in speech and writing • to segment words into phonemes for spelling • to investigate and classify words with the same sounds but different spellings	high-frequency words	• to read on sight and spell selected high-frequency words
Unit 10	ow ou	• to recognise the common spelling patterns for the vowel phoneme *ow* • to identify the phonemes in speech and writing • to segment the words into phonemes for spelling • to investigate and classify words with the same sounds but different spellings	syllables	• to discriminate, orally, syllables in multi-syllabic words
Unit 11	tch nch	• to discriminate, blend and spell consonant clusters *tch* and *nch*	same sound, different spelling pattern	• to investigate and classify words with the same sounds but different spellings
Unit 12	air	• to discriminate, spell and read the common spelling pattern for the vowel phoneme *air*	un prefix	• to spell words with the common prefix *un* to indicate the negative
Unit 13	are ear	• to discriminate, spell and read the common spelling patterns for the vowel phonemes *are* and *ear*	compound words	• to split familiar oral and written compound words into their component parts
Unit 14	or ore	• to discriminate, spell and read the common spelling patterns for the vowel phonemes *or* and *ore*	dis prefix	• to spell words with the common prefix *dis* to indicate the negative

Unit page	Spelling focus	Targets	Puzzle corner	Targets
Unit 15	aw au	• to discriminate, spell and read the common spelling patterns for the vowel phonemes *aw* and *au*.	syllables	• to discriminate syllables in multi-syllabic words
Unit 16	er	• to discriminate, spell and read the common spelling patterns for the vowel phoneme *er*	synonyms	• to use synonyms and other alternative words/ phrases that express the same or similar meanings
Unit 17	ir	• to discriminate, spell and read the common spelling patterns for the vowel phoneme *ir*	same spelling pattern, different sound	• to investigate words which have the same spelling patterns but different sounds
Unit 18	ur	• to discriminate, spell and read the common spelling patterns for the vowel phoneme *ur*	common irregular words	• to spell selected common irregular words
Unit 19	wh ph ch	• to read and spell words containing the consonant digraphs *wh, ph, ch* (as in 'Christopher')	ful suffix	• to spell words with the common suffix *ful*
Unit 20	wa	• to practise the letter pattern *wa*	high-frequency words	• to read on sight and spell high-frequency words
Unit 21	ear	• to discriminate, spell and read the most common spelling pattern for the vowel phoneme *ear*	ly suffix	• to spell words with the common suffix *ly*
Unit 22	ea	• to discriminate, spell and read the spelling pattern for the vowel phoneme *ea* (as in 'bread')	shades of meaning	• to collect and discuss similarities and shades of meaning

Unit notes, answers and copymasters
Units 1–22

Unit 1
ea
ee

Targets

- to secure identification, spelling and reading of long vowel digraphs *ea ee* in simple words
- to revise and extend the reading and spelling of words containing different spellings of the long vowel phoneme *ee*
- to use word ending *s* (plural) to support reading and spelling

Word list

pea	eat	bee	sheep
sea	heat	free	sleep
tea	meat	tree	sweets

Some other relevant words

flea

beat neat bleat treat cheat

fee pee tee wee

beep deep jeep peep seep weep asleep cheep
steep sweep

bean jeans lean mean clean

beam seam team cream dream gleam
ice cream scream steam stream

deal heal meal peal real seal zeal steal

beak leak teak creak freak speak

bead read lead plead

heap leap reap cheap

each beach peach reach teach

east beast feast least

heave leave weave

deed heed need reed breed greed speed
feet meet fleet street tweet
leek meek peek reek seek week creek
eel feel heel peel reel steel wheel
been keen seen green preen queen screen
breeze freeze squeeze sneeze wheeze

Relevant high-frequency words

been seen tree three

Pupil Book answers
Making words

1 tea **2** meat **3** sheep **4** tree
5 sweets **6** sea
A funny sentence using two **ea** words and two **ee** words.

Using words

steam steep
cream creep (cree)
tree treat
beach bee beep beam beat
tea teach tee team teat

Puzzle corner

dream stream scream ream cream bee tree
week seed leek

dreams streams screams reams creams bees
trees weeks seeds leeks

Copymaster/Homework answers
Unit 1A

jeans feet tree flea
Two **ea** words chosen by the child.
Two **ee** words chosen by the child.

Unit 1B

fleas beans spots bees sweets nails

Suggestions

- Write a few sentences on the board containing these vowel phonemes. Ask each group to choose a sentence, write it down and illustrate it.
- Draw the outline of two objects strongly associated with the vowel phonemes. Ask each child to write four words inside the outline of each object.
- The plural *s* has previously been covered in Book 1, Unit 13.
- Give the children a word (the plural form of which is taken by adding *s*), ask them to change it into the plural form and then write it into a sentence.

Name: _____   Date: _____

Match a word to the picture.

flea   tree   jeans   feet

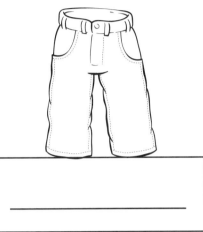

_____

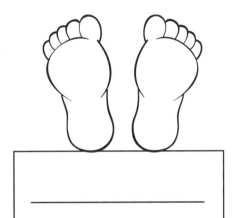

_____

_____

_____

Colour the pictures.

Write two more **ea** words.

_____   _____

Write two more **ee** words.

_____   _____

Name: _____   Date: _____

Plural means more than one thing.

Add an **s** to each of these words to make them plural.
The first one is done for you.

cat   **cats**

flea   _____

bean   _____

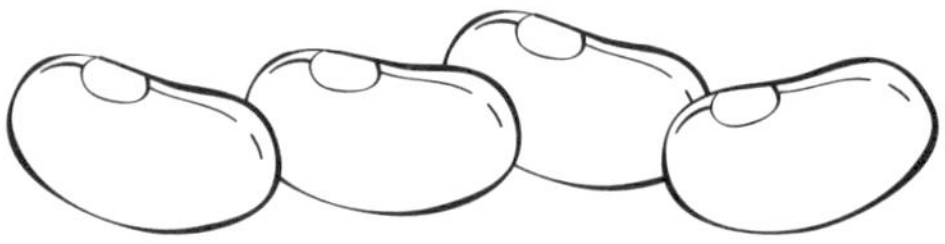

spot   _____

bee   _____

sweet   _____

nail   _____

Unit 2
ay
a–e
ai

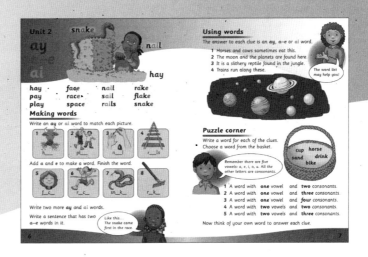

Targets

- to secure identification, spelling and reading of long vowel digraphs *ay a–e ai* in simple words
- to revise and extend the reading and spelling of words containing different spellings of the long vowel phoneme *ai*
- to secure understanding and use of the terms 'vowel' and 'consonant'

Word list

hay	face	nail	rake
pay	race	sail	flake
play	space	rails	snake

Some other relevant words

bay day gay jay lay may ray say way
ace lace pace place trace
bail fail hail jail mail pail rail tail
vail wail
brake shake

clay pray spray stray sway stay

age cage page rage sage wage stage

fade jade made blade grade shade spade
came fame game name same flame frame
shame
blaze graze
crate plate slate

aid aim
maid mail main
paid pail pain
raid rail rain
laid maid paid raid

Relevant high-frequency words

may way
came made make name take again
(These are practised in Copymaster 2B.)

Pupil Book answers

Making words

1 hay 2 play 3 nail 4 rails 5 face 6 race
7 snake 8 rake

Child adds two **ai** and two **ay** words of own.
Child's own sentence including two **a–e** words.

Using words

1 hay 2 space 3 snake 4 rails

Puzzle corner

1 cup 2 sand 3 drink 4 bike 5 horse
Child to write own words to match each clue.

Copymaster/Homework answers

Unit 2A

spade cage sail play

A funny sentence using an **ay**, **a–e** and **ai** word.

Unit 2B

Circles around vowels in: again came made
afraid Sunday.

Squares around consonants in: take name may
Wednesday make.

(Use the potential confusion with 'y' to secure the variable status of this letter as a semi-vowel.)

Suggestions

- Ask the children to make a wordsearch puzzle including as many *ay*, *a–e* and *ai* words as possible.

- Write sentences for children to complete by selecting the correct word from a list provided.

- Write the alphabet on the board. Ask children to read it out loud. Ask them to pick out and circle vowels and consonants in turn. Variations on this include asking children to stand when a vowel letter is reached, and to sit for consonants.

- Beware the 'semi-vowel' *y*. Explain that whilst every word requires a vowel, sometimes this can be *y* when it sounds like a long *i*, e.g. in 'by' or 'why'. This can be reinforced by shuffling an equal number of consonant and vowel letter cards. Add two *y* cards to the pack. The children who are dealt a vowel card are in the vowel team, and the same for consonants, but those with *y* cards can choose which team to join.

Name: _____   Date: _____

Match a word to the picture.

| cage | spade | sail | play |

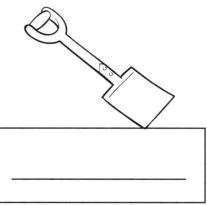

_____   _____

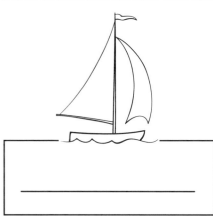

_____   _____

Colour the pictures.

Write a funny sentence using an **ay** word, an **a–e** word and an **ai** word.

_____

_____

_____

Unit 2B

Remember there are five vowels: **a e i o u**.
All the other letters are **consonants**.

In the first list draw a circle around each **vowel**.
In the second list draw a square around each
consonant.

List 1

again

came

made

afraid

Sunday

Like this: little

List 2

take

name

may

Wednesday

make

Like this: many

Unit 3
y
i–e
igh

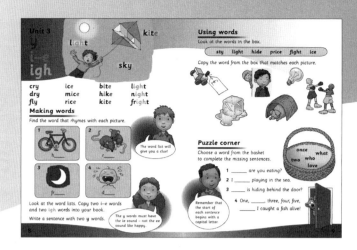

Targets

- to secure identification, spelling and reading of long vowel digraphs *y i–e igh* in simple words
- to revise and extend the reading and spelling of words containing different spellings of the long vowel phoneme *ie*
- to spell selected common irregular words

Word list

cry	ice	bite	light
dry	mice	hike	night
sky	rice	kite	fright

Some other relevant words

dice lice nice price slice spice twice
bike like mike spike strike
site spite
fine line mine nine pine vine wine shine

by my fry try shy sky spy

high sigh thigh
bright fight flight might sight slight tight

Relevant high-frequency words

by
live time
night

Pupil Book answers

Making words

1 hike **2** rice **3** fright **4** dry
Child copies two **i–e** and two **igh** words.
Child's own sentence including two **y** words where the 'y' is a long vowel sound.

Using words

1 price **2** hide **3** light **4** ice **5** sty **6** fight

Puzzle corner

1 What **2** love **3** Who **4** two, once

Copymaster/Homework answers

Unit 3A

Add the words to the picture – mice bike bite fly light
A sentence written about the picture.

Unit 3B

Write the following common irregular words three times – love said water half once

Suggestions

- Provide *y i–e igh* words on cards for children to sort into a table with *y i–e igh* columns. Let them choose three words to include in either one sentence or three sentences.

- In pairs, ask the children to take it in turns to draw an *i–e* word and an *igh* word and a *y* word. The child has to write the word their partner has drawn.

- Ask the children to write their own short story using the words in the *Puzzle corner* or Copymaster 3B.

Unit 3A

Add the **y**, **i–e** or **igh** words to the picture.

> mice   bike   bite   fly   light

Write a sentence about the picture.

_____

_____

_____

Unit 3B

Write each of these tricky words
three times in the balloons.
Use a different colour for each word.

half

_____

_____

_____

said

_____

_____

_____

love

_____

_____

_____

water

_____

_____

_____

once

_____

_____

_____

Unit 4
o–e
oa
ow

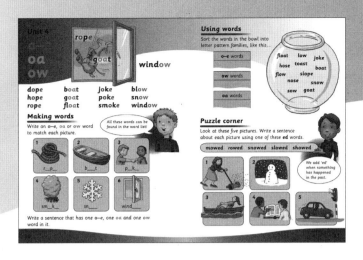

Targets

- to secure identification, spelling and reading of long vowel digraphs *o–e oa ow* in simple words
- to revise and extend the reading and spelling of words containing different spellings of the long vowel phoneme *oa*
- to use the word ending *ed* (past tense) to support reading and spelling

Word list

hope	boat	joke	blow
rope	goat	poke	snow
slope	float	smoke	window

Some other relevant words

cope dope mope grope
bone cone lone tone zone alone stone phone
woke bloke broke choke
hose nose pose rose chose close those
robe globe probe strobe

bow low mow row sow tow
flow grow show slow throw
bungalow tomorrow yellow

oak oat coat
coal foal
load loan moan foam roam groan
soak soap cloak coach croak
roast toast throat stoat road

Relevant high-frequency words

home over

Pupil Book answers
Making words

1 rope **2** boat **3** poke **4** smoke
5 snow **6** window
Child's own sentence including an **o–e**, an **oa** and an **ow** word.

Using words

o–e: joke hose slope nose
ow: low flow snow sow
oa: float toast boat goat

Puzzle corner

Child's own sentences including these words:
1 mowed **2** snowed **3** rowed **4** showed
5 slowed

Copymaster/Homework answers
Unit 4A

Picture labels – coat mole blow snow
A sentence using three words from the box.

Unit 4B

The following **ed** words added to the picture sentences – wished planted jumped played dropped covered.

Suggestions

- Give the children three words with each of the target spelling patterns. Spell one of the words in the three word group incorrectly. Ask the children to 'mark' your work and correct the spellings.
- Provide nine labelled pictures with *o–e*, *oa* and *ow* words for the children to sort into word pattern familes.
- The *ed* ending has previously been covered in Book 1, Unit 16.
- Ask children to find *ed* words from a book and write them down. Discuss the use of the *ed* ending and its use to describe events that have happened in the past.

Name: _____   Date: _____

Finish the word to label the picture.
Add **o–e**, **oa** or **ow** to these letters.

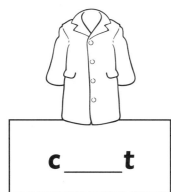

c____t

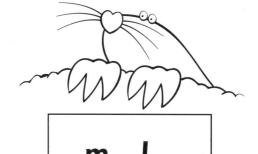

m__l__

bl____

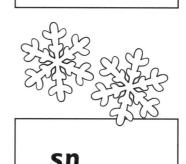

sn_____

Colour the pictures.

Choose one **o–e**, one **oa** and one **ow** word from this list.

> bone   grown   stone   hose   goat
> float   show   throw   yellow

Write them in a sentence.

_____

_____

_____

Name: _____   Date: _____

We add **ed** when something
has happened in the past.

Look at these five pictures.
Choose a word to finish each sentence.

dropped	planted	wished
jumped	played	covered

Alice _____ she had eaten her breakfast.

Yesterday Tom _____

a flower in the garden.

Misha _____ over

the puddle on her way to school.

The boys _____ football until it got dark.

Jess _____ her paint pot.

She was _____ in red paint!

Read the sentences out loud. Colour the pictures.

Unit 5
ew
ue
u–e
oo

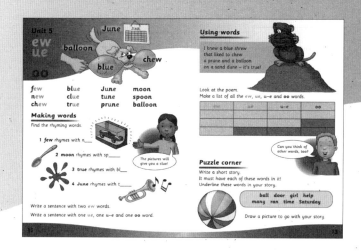

Targets

- to secure identification, spelling and reading of long vowel digraphs *ew ue u–e oo* in simple words
- to revise and extend the reading and spelling of words containing different spellings of the long vowel phoneme *oo*
- to read on sight and spell selected high-frequency words

Word list

few	blue	June	moon
new	clue	tune	spoon
chew	true	prune	balloon

Some other relevant words

dew mew yew Jew
blew brew crew drew grew screw shrew stew
threw

cue due sue cruel duel
glue rescue statue Tuesday

dune
cube tube
dude nude rude
mule rule ruler
cute mute flute brute absolute

boo moo too zoo
boom room zoom
bloom gloom broom
boot loot hoot root toot shoot scoot
food mood
fool pool tool spool stool
hoof roof proof
hoop loop scoop snoop swoop
noon soon

Relevant high-frequency words

new
too good
(The high-frequency words 'too' and 'good' give an opportunity to demonstrate that **oo** can have different sounds.)

Pupil Book answers
Making words

1 new **2** spoon **3** blue **4** tune
Child's own sentence including two **ew** words.
Child writes own sentence including words with **ue**, **u–e** and **oo** spelling pattern.

Using words

ew: knew shrew chew
ue: blue true
u–e: prune dune
oo: balloon

Puzzle corner

Child creates own illustrated story including the following words: ball door girl help many ran time Saturday.

Copymaster/Homework answers
Unit 5A

Sorting words into letter patterns.
ew: dew yew stew mew drew
ue: clue cue Tuesday glue blue
u–e: flute cube rule dune tube
oo: zoom moo pool hoof boom

Unit 5B

High-frequency words: bed push one tree laugh down

Suggestions

- Write a sentence on the board that includes each spelling pattern. Provide two words for each spelling pattern in the sentence. Children then have to choose the more appropriate word.

- Read the words from the *Using words* activity stressing the vowel phonemes as they are spoken. Think of other words in each pattern and write them on the board.

- Write the *Puzzle corner* words on flash cards for learning on sight for use in sentence construction. Make duplicates of the cards for playing Snap. You could also include the Copymaster 5B words, too.

Name: _____   Date: _____

The letters **ew**, **ue**, **u–e** and **oo** make the same sound.

Sort the words into the same spelling patterns.

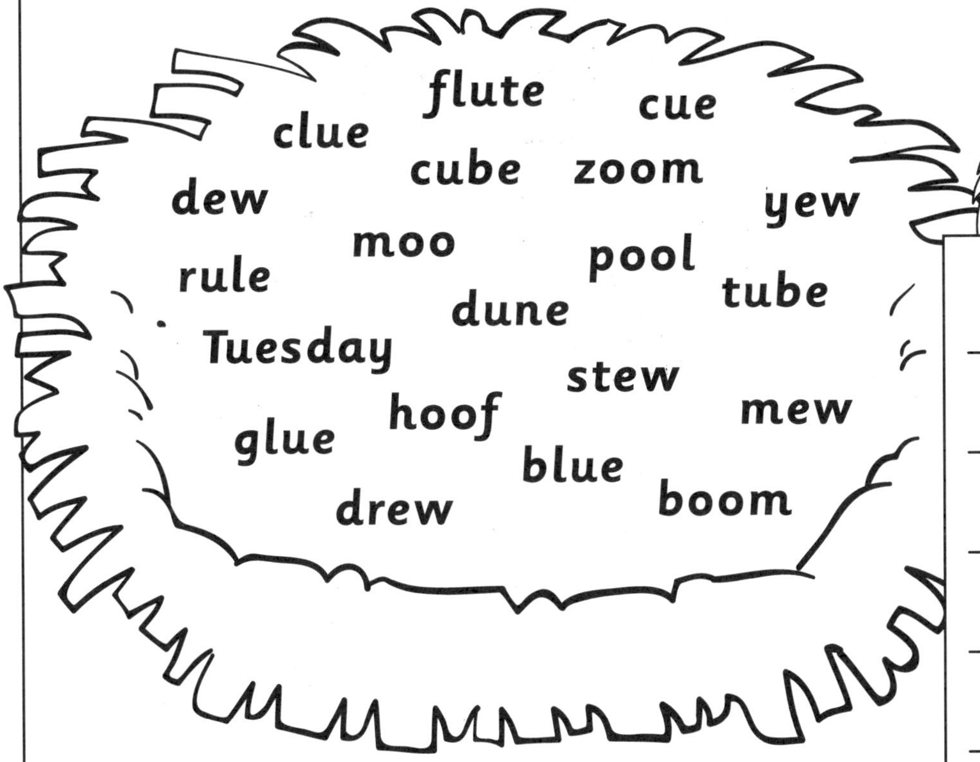

clue   flute   cue
dew   cube   zoom
       yew
rule   moo   pool
       dune   tube
Tuesday
       stew
glue   hoof   mew
   drew   blue   boom

ew words

_____
_____
_____
_____
_____

ue words

_____
_____
_____
_____
_____

u–e words

_____
_____
_____
_____
_____

oo words

_____
_____
_____
_____
_____

Name: _____   Date: _____

Write the word with the picture.

| laugh   tree   push   one   down   bed |

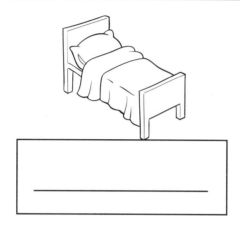

_____

_____

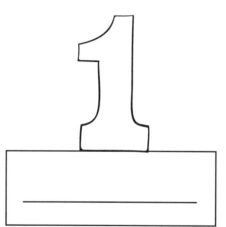

_____

_____

_____

_____

Colour the pictures.

Unit 6
ck

Targets
- to secure the spelling of words ending in *ck*
- to use the word ending *ing* to support reading and spelling

Word list

back	deck	kick	duck
rack	neck	lick	muck
sack	peck	tick	clock

Some other relevant words

lack pack
pick sick wick
dock lock rock sock
luck suck tuck

Relevant high-frequency words

back

Pupil Book answers
Making words

The words they can find in the picture are:
kick sack duck back lick neck.
Child draws picture to illustrate another **ck** word.

Using words

1 back **2** peck **3** lick **4** tick
5 lock **6** duck

Puzzle corner

1 pecking **2** locking **3** sucking **4** kicking

Copymaster/Homework answers

Unit 6A
sock neck duck sack
Three **ck** words chosen by the child.

Unit 6B
watering packing pushing eating jumping
fighting buying holding

Suggestions
- Brainstorm *ck* words. Ask the children to draw a funny picture with four to six *ck* words in it. Ask them to label the picture.
- Ask the children to find as many *ck* words as they can in their reading books. Ask them to write the words down.
- Invite selected children to mime an action – running on the spot, jumping up and down, sleeping, laughing, whispering, etc. Ask the children to write down the *ing* sentence that describes what the children are doing, e.g. Ellie is sleeping.
- The *ing* participle has previously been covered in Book 1, Unit 21.

Unit 6A

Match the word to the picture.

| sack   duck   neck   sock |

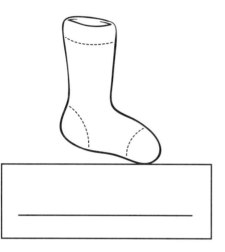

_____

_____

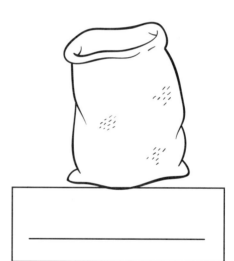

_____

_____

Colour the pictures.

Here are my three words...
rocking, wick, lick

Write three more **ck** words.

_____   _____   _____

Unit 6B

Look at these picture clues.
What are they doing?

Write each word.
Add **ing** to put each word in the **present tense**.

Remember that present tense means it is happening now!

jump   push   water   fight   eat   buy   pack   hold

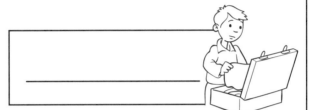

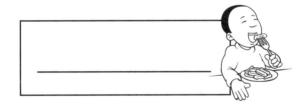

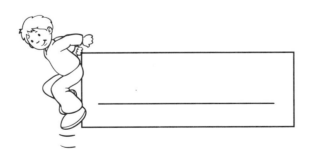

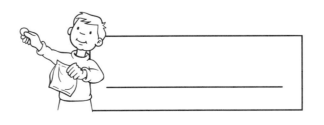

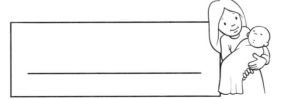

Unit 7

u

oo

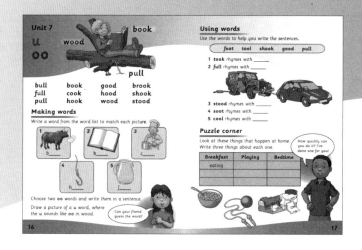

Targets

- to recognise the common spelling patterns for the vowel phoneme *oo*
- to identify the phonemes in speech and writing
- to segment the words into phonemes for spelling
- to investigate and classify words with the same sounds but different spellings
- to learn to spell significant words of personal interest

Word list

bull	book	good	brook
full	cook	hood	shook
pull	hook	wood	stood

Some other relevant words

look rook crook
foot soot
bully fully pulley
useful careful faithful dreadful thoughtful
wonderful
usefully carefully faithfully dreadfully
thoughtfully wonderfully

Relevant high-frequency words

put pull
took

Pupil Book answers

Making words

1 bull **2** book **3** cook
4 hook **5** full
Child's own sentence including two **oo** words.
Illustration of child's selected **u** word.

Using words

1 shook **2** pull **3** good
4 foot **5** tool

Puzzle corner

Three things that happen at breakfast, playing and bedtime. Individual answers.

Copymaster/Homework answers

Unit 7A

cook foot bully bull
One **u** and one **oo** word chosen from the box and written in a sentence.

Unit 7B

A label for each word collection
School – picture book teacher pencil
Shopping – basket tin oranges money
Holiday – spade sand sea bucket

Suggestions

- It is critical to spend as much time as necessary to ensure the children appreciate the different phonemes associated with the *oo* grapheme. Make large flashcards of ten *oo* words, five from each *oo* group. Invite ten children to hold the words so that they can be read by all the children, practise reading the words and then ask the class to organise the ten children into the two sound groups.

- With selected children, introduce the frequently used words 'could', 'should' and 'would'. These include the *oo* phoneme represented, unusually, by *ou*.

- Start a class word display which focuses on significant topics of general and particular interest. Link this with the keeping and collecting of words for personal word books.

Unit 7A

Finish the word to label the picture.

Add **u** or **oo** to these letters.

c___k

f___t

b__lly

b__ll

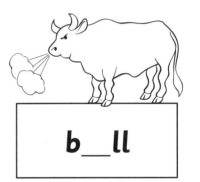

Colour the pictures.

Choose one **oo** word and one **u** word from the box and write them in a sentence.

book   look   crook   full   pull   bully

_____

_____

_____

_____

Name: _____   Date: _____

Draw a line to each picture and
label it. Use the words in each pot to help.

School

picture
book
teacher
pencil

Shopping

basket
oranges tin
money

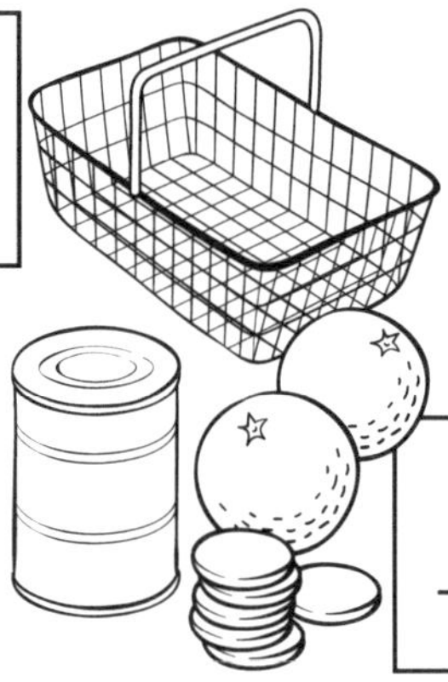

Holiday

spade
sand
sea bucket

Colour your favourite picture.

Unit 8

ar

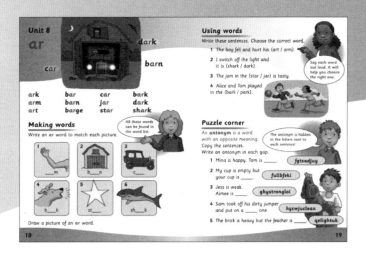

Targets

- to recognise the common spelling patterns for the vowel phoneme *ar*
- to identify the phonemes in speech and writing
- to segment the words into phonemes for spelling
- to investigate and classify words with the same sounds but different spellings
- to introduce the use of antonyms: collect, discuss differences of meaning and their spelling

Word list

ark	bar	car	bark
arm	barn	jar	dark
ark	barge	star	shark

Some other relevant words

card cart
dart
hard harm harp
far
lark mark park spark
farm harm charm
chart part start smart
card hard yard
large charge

Relevant high-frequency words

are

Pupil Book answers
Making words

1 arm **2** barn **3** car **4** bark
5 star **6** shark
A picture of an **ar** word.

Using words

1 arm **2** dark **3** jar **4** park

Puzzle corner

1 sad **2** full **3** strong
4 clean **5** light

Copymaster/Homework answers
Unit 8A

car dark card tart star
Child writes own sentence including an **ar** word.

Unit 8B

The antonym pairs are:
new – old   good – bad   do – don't   love – hate
more – less   can – can't   night – day.

Suggestions

- This phoneme is reasonably straightforward for most children, and building collections of *ar* words can be a productive activity for nearly all.

- In some regions dialect can cause a problem with words such as path, bath, past and fast in which the vowel phoneme sounds as though it 'needs' an *r*. These words can be taken as a small group and taught separately if appropriate.

- Another group of related words which might be tackled with those children who have grasped the main target pattern is the *are* family, e.g. care, fare.

- Note that all Copymaster B 'rocket' words are significant high-frequency words. This work can be extended by making a class collection of antonyms – children enjoy using the technical language and also the word play associated with finding 'matching' words.

Name: _____   Date: _____

Unit 8A

Finish the sentences with the **ar** words.

car   tart   card   star   dark

   Sundip went to school in a _____.

Jess was afraid of the _____.

   Alice sent James a _____
for his birthday.

A jam _____ is a very tasty cake.

Twinkle twinkle little _____,
how I wonder what you are.

Think of your own sentence using an **ar** word.

_____

_____

Draw a picture of it.

Unit 8B

An **antonym** is a word with
the opposite meaning to another word.

Draw a line from the word in each
rocket to its antonym in a star.

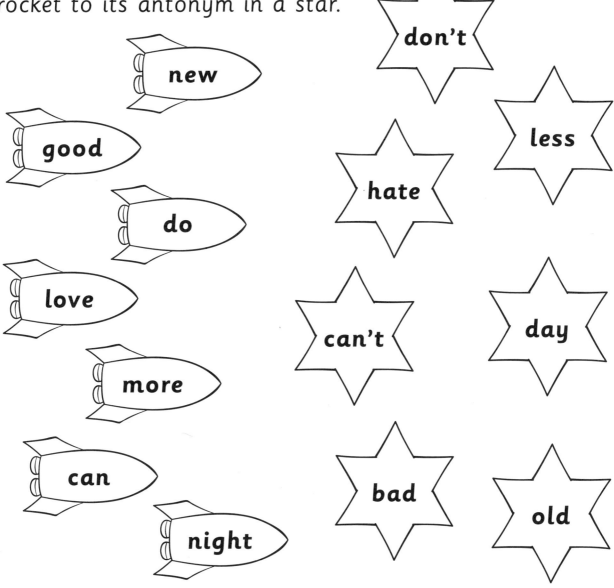

Use a rocket word and its star word in a sentence.

_____

_____

Unit 9
oy
oi

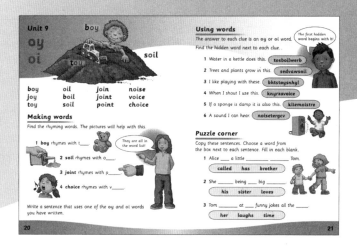

Targets

- to recognise the common spelling patterns for the vowel phoneme *oy*
- to identify the phonemes in speech and writing
- to segment the words into phonemes for spelling
- to investigate and classify words with the same sounds but different spellings
- to read on sight and spell selected high-frequency words

Word list

boy	oil	join	noise
joy	boil	joint	voice
toy	soil	point	choice

Some other relevant words

coy

enjoy destroy annoy royal loyal oyster

spoil toil

coin

moist poise poison

Relevant high-frequency words

boy

Pupil Book answers

Making words

1 toy **2** oil **3** point **4** voice

Child's own sentence that includes an **oy** and an **oi** word.

Using words

1 boils **2** soil **3** toys **4** voice
5 moist **6** noise

Puzzle corner

The sentences should read:

1 Alice has a little brother called Tom.
2 She loves being his big sister.
3 Tom laughs at her funny jokes all the time.

Copymaster/Homework answers

Unit 9A

boy toy voice boil oink oink

Child's own sentence using an **oy** and an **oi** word

Unit 9B

The high-frequency words made are –
again because half if next water took people.

Child's own sentence incorporating three of these words.

Suggestions

- These word groups provide a helpful opportunity to practise looking for common rime structures (the 'rime' being the part of the word comprising the vowel phoneme and following consonant(s)). Thus a useful group or class activity is to write the rime patterns *oy*, *oil* and *oin* on the board and then collect words to match each set, i.e. oy: boy, toy, coy, joy, Roy oil: oil, boil, toil, soil, spoil oin: coin, join.

- A helpful teaching point, when appropriate, is that the *oi* spelling pattern never appears at the end of a word. By contrast, *oy* occasionally appears medially, notably when preceding a suffix (e.g. employed).

- Copymaster 9B can be adjusted for difficulty by the teacher completing some of the connections before the child commences work, thus eliminating some of the options.

Name: _____   Date: _____

Unit 9A

Finish the sentences with an **oy** or **oi** word.

| boy   oink   toy   voice   boil |

Dave is not a girl. He is a _____.

Emily played with her favourite _____ all day.

Joe is a good singer. He has a lovely _____.

To make a cup of tea we _____ the water.

The noise a pig makes is _____ _____!

Think of your own sentence using an **oy** and an **oi** word.

_____

_____

Draw a picture of it.

Name: _____ Date: _____

Make a word.

Match the letters by drawing a line between them.
Write the word. The first one is done for you.

ag	lf
be	ter
ha	ain
i	xt
ne	ok
wa	cause
to	ple
peo	f

_____

_____

_**again**_____

_____

_____

_____

_____

Clue… One word you can drink!

Write a sentence using three
of the words you have made.

_____

_____

_____

Unit 10
ow
ou

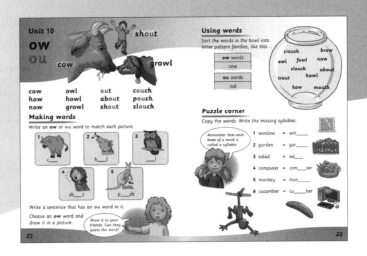

Targets

- to recognise the common spelling patterns for the vowel phoneme *ow*
- to identify the phonemes in speech and writing
- to segment the words into phonemes for spelling
- to investigate and classify words with the same sounds but different spellings
- to discriminate, orally, syllables in multi-syllabic words

Word list

cow	owl	out	couch
how	howl	about	pouch
now	growl	shout	slouch

Some other relevant words

bow row sow wow brow
fowl prowl scowl
down crown brown frown gown
crowd tower power shower
bound found hound mound sound wound
count mount
ounce bounce pounce
crouch
mouse house
mouth south

Relevant high-frequency words

how now down
out our about house

Pupil Book answers
Making words

1 cow **2** howl **3** owl
4 shout **5** pouch
Child's own sentence including an **ou** word.
An illustration of an **ow** word.

Using words

ow words: brow owl fowl now howl how
ou words: crouch slouch about trout mouth

Puzzle corner

The syllable answer is emboldened.

1 win**dow** **2** gar**den** **3** sal**ad**
4 comp**u**ter **5** mon**key** **6** cu**cum**ber

Copymaster/Homework answers
Unit 10A

shower bounce mouse owl
The table completed by adding an **ow** or **ou** word
e.g. cow brown pound pouch.

Unit 10B

Syllables divided as follows:
pil/low hun/gry bub/ble po/ta/to fun/fair
oc/to/pus

Suggestions

- Following the work in the previous unit, here is another good opportunity to work on rime patterns, particularly the *ow*, *own*, *owl* and *ound* sets of words.

- Whilst the *ou* and *ow* patterns are important graphemes, both have their complications when teaching the related phonemes, e.g. cow / throw. Especially frustrating for the teacher is that the most frequently used *ou* words are 'irregular', e.g. could, would, should, you, your, through, thought.

- The key to understanding syllables is that each syllable must contain a vowel sound – a useful extension to teaching about vowels and consonants.

Unit 10A

Look at the pictures.

Match a word to each picture.

mouse   shower   bounce   owl

_____

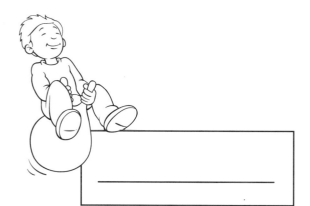

_____

_____

_____

Finish the table.

Add an **ow** or **ou** word to each rhyming family.

bow	down	bound	slouch
now	crown	mound	crouch

Name: _____   Date: _____

Remember that the beats in a word are called **syllables**.

Unit 10B

Draw a line to divide each word into syllables, like this.

yellow   **y e l/l o w**

pillow   **p i l l o w**

hungry   **h u n g r y**

bubble   **b u b b l e**

potato   **p o t a t o**

funfair   **f u n f a i r**

octopus   **o c t o p u s**

• Unit 10B • syllables • Spelling Book 2

Unit 11
tch
nch

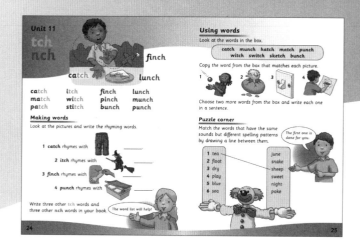

Targets

- to discriminate, blend and spell consonant clusters *tch* and *nch*
- to investigate and classify words with the same sounds but different spellings

Word list

catch	itch	finch	lunch
match	witch	pinch	munch
patch	stitch	bunch	punch

Some other relevant words

hatch snatch scratch
bitch ditch hitch pitch switch
fetch stretch
crutch hutch
bench drench trench wench

Relevant high-frequency words

No relevant words.

Pupil Book answers

Making words

1 patch **2** witch **3** pinch **4** lunch
Child adds three **tch** and three **nch** words.

Using words

1 catch **2** hatch **3** switch **4** sketch
Child uses two of the words in own sentences.

Puzzle corner

1 tea – sheep **2** float – poke
3 dry – night **4** play – snake
5 blue – June **6** sea – sweet

Copymaster/Homework answers

Unit 11A

The following labels added to the picture – catch itch munch lunch witch pinch.
A sentence about the picture.

Unit 11B

tune rope night fluke hood
A sentence that has two words with the same sound spelt differently.

Suggestions

- It is worth revisiting the *ch* consonant digraph before commencing work on this unit (see Book 1, Unit 7). In doing so, it can be noted that *ch* at the end of a word is more often than not accompanied by a *t* or *n*, the main exceptions being 'rich', 'much' and 'such'. Write a selection of words ending in *ch* on the board, invite selected children to underline the letter before the *ch* and from this draw out the importance of the *tch* and *nch* patterns.

- Words including the *tch* and *nch* clusters are regular when adding the suffixes *ed* and *ing*. A useful supplementary activity revisiting earlier work on suffixes might therefore be undertaken at this time.

- The *Puzzle corner* activity gives an opportunity to revisit the different graphemic representations for the main vowel sounds. This type of activity can be turned into a simple game, encouraging the children (perhaps for homework) to make collections of words with the same vowel sound but differing spelling patterns.

Unit 11A

Add **tch** or **nch** words to the picture.
Colour the picture.

> catch   itch   munch   lunch   witch   pinch

Write a sentence about the picture.

_____

_____

_____

_____

Name: _____   Date: _____

Unit 11B

Write the word from the box
that includes the same sound spelt differently.

rope   flake   hood   tune   night

The first is done
to help you.

chew   tune

blow   _____

ice   _____

hay   _____

bull   _____

Write a sentence that has two words with the same
sound spelt differently.

_____

_____

_____

Unit 12
air

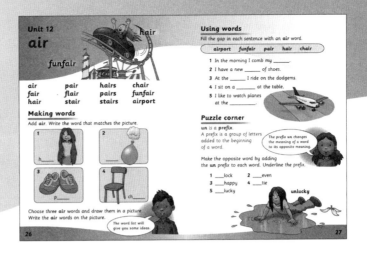

Targets

- to discriminate, spell and read the common spelling pattern for the vowel phoneme *air*
- to spell words with the common prefix *un* to indicate the negative

Word list

air	pair	hairs	chair
fair	flair	pairs	funfair
hair	stair	stairs	airport

Some other relevant words

lair

dairy hairy

repair

upstairs downstairs

Relevant high-frequency words

No relevant words.

Pupil Book answers

Making words

1 hair **2** air **3** pair **4** chair

Child's own annotated picture using three **air** words.

Using words

1 hair **2** pair **3** funfair

4 chair **5** airport

Puzzle corner

1 unlock **2** uneven **3** unhappy

4 untie **5** unlucky

Copymaster/Homework answers

Unit 12A

f + air = fair

st + air = stair

h + air = hair

rep + air = repair

h + air + y = hairy

air + port = airport

fun + fair = funfair

A picture of an **air** word.

Unit 12B

The **un** words labelling the pictures are – unpack untie uncover untidy unzip undress.

Child's own sentence using an **un** prefixed word.

Suggestions

- Before commencing this unit it will probably be advisable to revisit the *ai* letter pattern (see Book 1, Unit 19).
- Whilst the *air* pattern is a natural extension of work on the *ai* phoneme, *air* and *are* often represent the same phoneme, and in frequently used words, e.g. bare, care, dare, fare, hare, mare, rare, glare, stare, scare, snare, share. This might offer opportunities to introduce some simple homophones.
- The negative prefix *un* gives the chance to revise work in earlier units on antonyms (e.g. happy, unhappy) and, for those ready to take things further, to introduce synonyms (e.g. unhappy/sad).

Name: _____   Date: _____

Finish the word sums.

f + air = _____

st + _____ = stair

_____ + air = hair

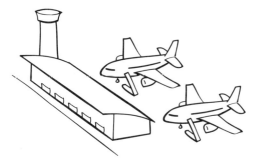

rep + air = _____

h + _____ + y = hairy

air + _____ = airport

fun + fair = _____

Draw a picture of an **air** word.

Ask someone to write down what they think it is.

Unit 12B

The prefix **un** changes the meaning of a word to its opposite meaning.

Write the **un** word with the picture.

| untidy | uncover | untie | unzip | unpack | undress |

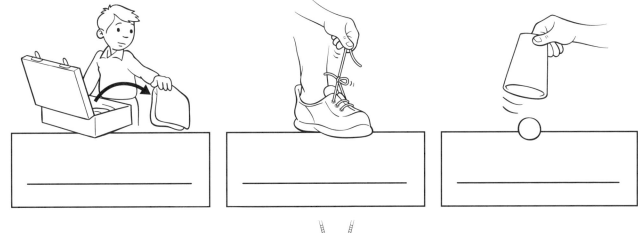

_____ _____ _____

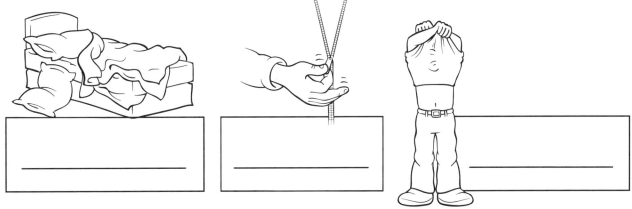

_____ _____ _____

Write a sentence using an **un** word.

_____

_____

_____

Unit 13
are
ear

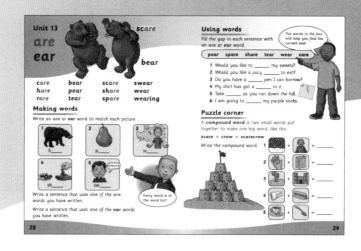

Targets

- to discriminate, spell and read the common spelling patterns for the vowel phonemes *are* and *ear*
- to split familiar oral and written compound words into their component parts

Word list

care	bear	scare	swear
hare	pear	share	wear
rare	tear	spare	wearing

Some other relevant words

bare dare fare mare
glare stare snare
swearing

Relevant high-frequency words

No relevant words.

Pupil Book answers

Making words

1 bear **2** pear **3** scare **4** share **5** swear
Child writes own sentences using an **are** and **ear** word.

Using words

1 share **2** pear **3** spare **4** tear
5 care **6** wear

Puzzle corner

1 snowman **2** handbag **3** sandcastle
4 toothbrush **5** teaspoon

Copymaster/Homework answers

Unit 13A

Match the word to the picture – scare pear
bear hare
One **are** and one **ear** word written in a sentence.

Unit 13B

The compound words are – homework
skateboard football bedroom matchbox lipstick
shoelace or shoebox

Suggestions

- Before commencing this unit it will probably be advisable to revisit the *ar* and *ea* letter patterns. In particular it is important to draw out that in this unit the children will be working with the less common phonemic form of the letter patterns, i.e. the *ear* in wear not in hear, and the *ar* in share not in car.

- Clearly, the work in this unit follows naturally on from Unit 12, to which reference should be made, probably in discussion when the work is finished.

- Before undertaking the work on compound words it may be necessary to write the component words on the board, e.g. snow, man, castle, etc.

- As a follow-up activity, give the children a word and challenge them (possibly for homework) to find as many related compound words as they are able, e.g. bed (bedroom, bedtime, etc.).

Name: _____   Date: _____

Match the word to the picture.

bear   hare   pear   scare

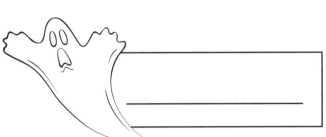

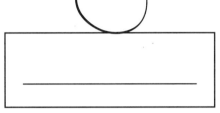

_____

_____

_____

_____

Write a sentence with one **are** word and one **ear** word.

Choose from these words.

care   stare   share

bear   tear   wear

_____

_____

_____

_____

Unit 13B

Two small words put together to make one big word is called a **compound word**.

The first one is done to help you.

Join the two words together to make a big word. Write the word. The first one is done for you.

light	ball	_____
home	board	_____
skate	box	_____
foot	house	**lighthouse**
bed	room	_____
match	work	_____
lip	lace	_____
shoe	stick	_____

Colour the lighthouse.

Unit 14
or
ore

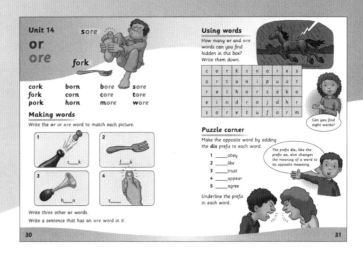

Targets

- to discriminate, spell and read the common spelling patterns for the vowel phonemes *or* and *ore*
- to spell words with the common prefix *dis* to indicate the negative

Word list

cork	born	bore	sore
fork	corn	core	tore
pork	horn	more	wore

Some other relevant words

or for force
cord ford lord
stork
door moor
form storm
gorge
morn torn worn
sword sworn scorn
fort port sort snort sport short
porch torch scorch
north author order
ore store score snore swore shore before

Relevant high-frequency words

or more door

Pupil Book answers
Making words

1 cork **2** fork **3** horn **4** sore
Child writes three further **or** words.
Child's own sentence including an **ore** word.

Using words

There are nine hidden words:
cork snore horse sore form core ore
snort storm.

Puzzle corner

1 disobey **2** dislike **3** distrust
4 disappear **5** disagree

Copymaster/Homework answers
Unit 14A

Drawing a line from each bird to **or** or **ore** nest.
or words are: born order cork storm
ore words are: snore more shore before
Pupil writes own funny sentence using **or** and **ore** words.

Unit 14B

un or **dis** prefixes to complete each sentence – unlucky disappear untie dislike unlock.
Write a sentence using one of: disagree unhappy disobey undo.

Suggestions

- Unlike the earlier work using *ar/are* vowel phonemes, *or/ore* have no difference in sound – a point to share with the children.
- This unit is the first of a pair (with Unit 15) considering similar phonemes represented by *aw* and *au*.
- The negative prefix *un* should be revisited as an introduction to the vocabulary work in this unit (see Unit 12). As a related activity, themed artwork might be undertaken with the child asked to incorporate into a picture positive and negative aspects of a chosen root word, e.g. like/dislike, happy/unhappy, obey/disobey.

Name: _____ Date: _____

Read each word.

Draw a line to take each bird to its **ore** or **or** nest.

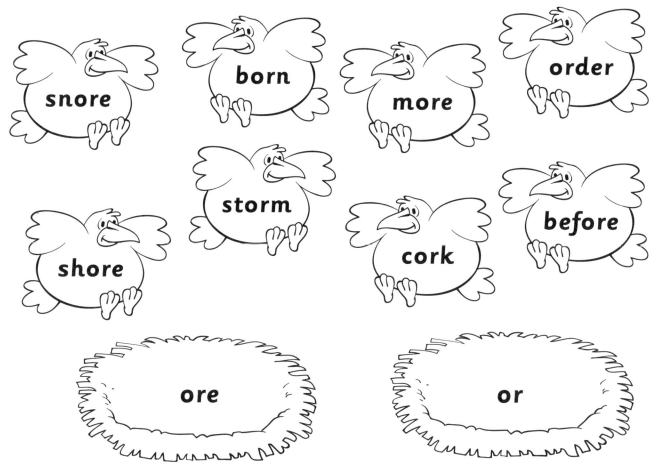

Write a funny sentence using as many **or** and **ore** words as you can.

_____

_____

_____

_____

Name: _____ Date: _____

The prefix **dis**, like the prefix **un**, changes the meaning of a word to its opposite.

Choose an **un** or **dis** prefix to complete each sentence.

(**un   dis**)

Manesh tripped over the kerb. He was very ___lucky.

I saw the ghost ___appear.

Please can you ___tie my shoelaces?

I ___like getting wet in the rain.

Please can you ___lock the door?

Write a sentence using one of these words.

(**disagree   unhappy   disobey   undo**)

```
_____

_____

_____

_____
```

Unit 15
aw
au

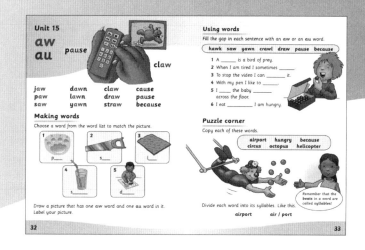

Targets

- to discriminate, spell and read the common spelling patterns for the vowel phonemes *aw* and *au*

- to discriminate syllables in multi-syllabic words

Word list

jaw	dawn	claw	cause
paw	lawn	draw	pause
saw	yawn	straw	because

Some other relevant words

raw thaw
fawn drawn prawn
bawl crawl trawl sprawl shawl
awful hawk

caught taught daughter
sauce August autumn
author launch naughty fault saucer

Relevant high-frequency words

saw because

Pupil Book answers

Making words

1 paw **2** saw **3** lawn **4** straw **5** draw
Child's annotated illustration incorporating an **aw** and **au** word.

Using words

1 hawk **2** yawn **3** pause **4** draw
5 saw, crawl **6** because

Puzzle corner

The words divided into syllables look like this:
air / port
hun / gry
be / cause
cir / cus
oc / to / pus
he / li / cop / ter

Copymaster/Homework answers

Unit 15A

Writing **aw** or **au** 'bee' words into the correct beehives.

aw words are: fawn bawl awful draw

au words are: August sauce caught launch

A funny sentence using **aw** and **au** words.

Unit 15B

Matching syllables – brother garden sister princess circus purple kicking

birthday = 2 syllables   tummy = 2   Saturday = 3
cat = 1

Suggestions

- Taken with the graphemes in the previous unit, the *aw* grapheme is in several words with a very similar, if not identical, phoneme (sound) to other words i.e. if not actual homophones, certainly close enough to cause confusion. Work with the following sets of words will intrigue some children and make for more accurate spelling:

  saw sore; paw poor pour; for four; ore or; flaw floor; horse hoarse; more moor

- As noted in Unit 10, the key to understanding syllables is that each syllable must contain a vowel sound – a useful extension to teaching about vowels and consonants.

Name: _____   Date: _____

The letter patterns **aw** and **au**
can make similar sounds.
Write each word in the correct hive.

awful

fawn   bawl

sauce   caught

August   launch

draw

au   aw

Write a sentence using as many
aw and **au** words as you can.

Can you write a
funny sentence?

_____

_____

_____

_____

Unit 15B

A **syllable** is a part of a word that can be sounded by itself.

Make a word.
Match a syllable in the first column to a syllable in the second column.
The first one is done for you.

broth	den	_____
gar	cess	_____
sis	er	**brother**
prin	ter	_____
cir	ing	_____
pur	ple	_____
kick	cus	_____

Say these words out loud. Write how many syllables you can hear.

birthday _____

tummy _____

Saturday _____

cat _____

Unit 16
er

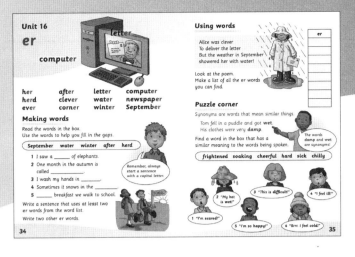

Targets

- to discriminate, spell and read the common spelling patterns for the vowel phoneme *er*
- to use synonyms and other alternative words/ phrases that express the same or similar meanings

Word list

her	after	letter	computer
herd	clever	water	newspaper
ever	corner	winter	September

Some other relevant words

herb kerb
germ fern term
every
brother sister mother father
litter better butter
slipper hopper shopper chopper supper stopper
digger flipper mixer
boxer cleaner flower paper monster shorter
taller trouser

Relevant high-frequency words

her were after over water sister brother
another

Pupil Book answers

Making words

1 herd **2** September **3** water
4 winter **5** After
Child's own sentence incorporating two **er** words from the word list.
Child to write two other **er** words.

Using words

The **er** words in the poem are as follows:
clever deliver letter weather winter
her water.

Puzzle corner

The word (synonym) in the box that sounds like the words being spoken are as follows:
1 frightened **2** soaking **3** hard
4 sick **5** cheerful **6** chilly

Copymaster/Homework answers

Unit 16A

Add **er** to the word. The **er** words are:
flower sister monster trouser butter digger
her ever
Child's sentence using an **er** word, with a picture.

Unit 16B

The synonym pairs are – big/large eat/chew
cold/icy small/little smash/break leap/jump
coat/jacket enjoy/like.
A sentence using two synonyms.

Suggestions

- This phoneme is technically known as the schwa vowel. In a few instances *er* appears as a straightforward vowel digraph within a word (e.g. herd), but *er* is most commonly found at the end of a word, where it is pronounced as a short, gentle 'grunt'.

- This unit provides an opportunity to follow up work on syllables from the previous unit as *er* is often preceded by a double consonant, e.g. butter. In such two-syllable words, the division is normally taken between the double letters, i.e. but / ter.

- Revisit antonyms (see Units 8, 12, 14) to remind children about opposites. Then discuss how our writing can be made more interesting if we try to avoid using the same word repeatedly.

Add **er** to make a word.
Write the word in the space.

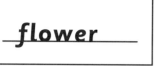

flower

flow   sist

monst   trous

butt   digg

h   ev

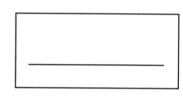

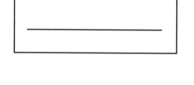

Think of your own sentence using an **er** word.

Draw a picture of it.

Name: ______________________________ Date: ______________

Unit 16B

Synonyms are words that mean similar things.

Draw a line from each word in the beehive to its synonym in the bees.
The first one is done for you.

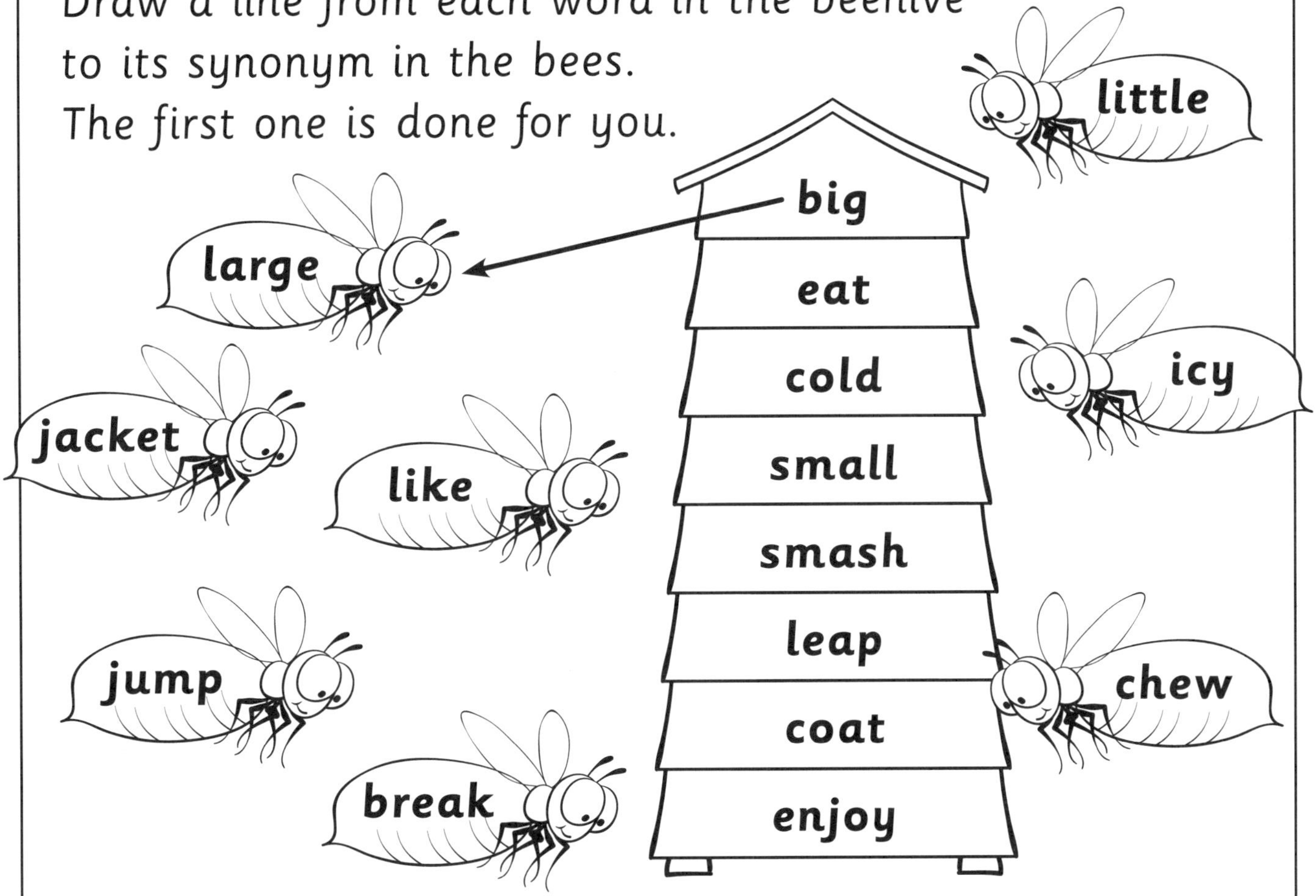

little
big
large
eat
cold
icy
jacket
like
small
smash
leap
jump
chew
coat
break
enjoy

Write a sentence using two synonyms.

____

____

____

____

Unit 17
ir

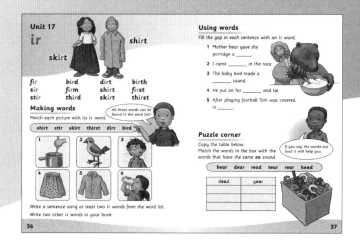

Targets

- to discriminate, spell and read the common spelling patterns for the vowel phoneme *ir*
- to investigate words which have the same spelling patterns but different sounds

Word list

fir	bird	dirt	birth
sir	firm	shirt	first
stir	third	skirt	thirst

Some other relevant words

flirt squirt circus
girl swirl twirl thirsty
chirp birch mirth

Relevant high-frequency words

first girl

Pupil Book answers

Making words

1 stir **2** bird **3** dirt **4** skirt
5 shirt **6** thirst
Child's sentence incorporating two **ir** words.
Child to write two other **ir** words.

Using words

1 stir **2** first or third **3** chirp
4 shirt **5** dirt

Puzzle corner

dead	year
head	tear
read	rear
bear	dear
tear	read

Copymaster/Homework answers

Unit 17A

s + ir = sir
g + ir + l = girl
ch + irp = chirp
sk + irt = skirt
b + ir + d = bird
st + ir = stir
bir + th = birth
f + ir = fir
Child to choose two **ir** words and write them in a sentence.

Unit 17B

food	book
town	mow
head	tea
would	cloud
swan	can

Suggestions

- The spelling patterns or digraphs *ir*, *er*, *ur* and *ar* are sometimes referred to as the 'r vowels'. The first three (except when *er* is a schwa vowel – see Unit 16) are very similar in sound and, for an emerging speller, tricky to differentiate!

- Interestingly, there are relatively few *ir* root words, as will be noted from the lists above. So if the children learn these they will know only to use *ir* for these words; other words with the phoneme will probably be spelt with *ur*. As noted previously, *er* is also unusual in a medial position, though very common in a final position in a root word (i.e. word without suffixes).

- The vowel digraph *ea* can represent several different sounds. The *Puzzle corner* and Copymaster 17B are primarily starting points to explore any vowel graphemes that can represent more than one phoneme.

Unit 17A

Finish the word sums.

s + ir = _____

g + _____ + l = girl

_____ + irp = chirp

sk + irt = _____

b + ir + d = _____

st + _____ = stir

_____ + th = birth

f + ir = _____

Choose two of these **ir** words and write them in a sentence.

girl bird first circus shirt skirt

_____

_____

_____

_____

Name: _____ Date: _____

Match the words that have the same spelling patterns but different sounds by drawing a line between them.

Write both words.

The first one is done for you.

food   mow   _____/_____

town   cloud   _____/_____

head   can   _____/_____

would   book   __*food*___/__*book*___

swan   tea   _____/_____

Colour the picture.

Label the picture with **food** and **book**.

Unit 18
ur

Targets

- to discriminate, spell and read the common spelling patterns for the vowel phoneme *ur*
- to spell selected common irregular words

Word list

burn	fur	hurt	curse
turn	curl	surf	nurse
churn	hurl	turf	purse

Some other relevant words

urn

burp slurp

spurt

purple

urge surge

curve

burnt

burst

church

return

Relevant high-frequency words

No relevant words.

Pupil Book answers

Making words

1 fur **2** curl **3** surf **4** turf
5 nurse **6** purse

Child to incorporate two **ur** words in a sentence and draw a picture of an **ur** word.

Using words

1 curl **2** churn **3** nurse
4 surf **5** surge

Puzzle corner

Four common irregular words in the wordsearch:
said half water two.

Copymaster/Homework answers

Unit 18A

church surf burst nurse

Child's own sentence with two **ur** words.

Unit 18B

Common irregular words in this order – Do have Monday February want little

Pupil writes a funny sentence using two words from the list.

Suggestions

- This is the third in a suite of units with a common phoneme. As will be noticed by glancing at the word lists, there is no easy rule to help the children differentiate whether to use *er*, *ir* or *ur* – except that *er* is the most frequent of the three at the end of a root word.

- The only way to learn the spellings of the common irregular words is by rote. Whilst teachers will have their favoured methods, the lists of those most frequently used in the *Look, Say, Cover, Write, Check* section at the back of this book will be helpful. Also, try introducing the notion of mnemonics where this works for particular children.

Unit 18A

Match the word to the picture.

burst   surf   nurse   church

_____   _____

_____   _____

Colour the pictures.

Write a sentence with two of these **ur** words.

burp   hurt   purple   turn   purse   fur

_____

_____

_____

_____

Unit 18B

Choose a word to complete each sentence.

Write the word again at the end of the sentence.

> **Monday   want   little   have   Do   February**

_____ you like playing in the sea?   _____

I _____ to eat my tea now.   _____

_____ is the first day of the week. _____

After the month of January comes _____.

_____

Do you _____ to play football now?   _____

I would like a _____ bit more please. _____

Write a funny sentence using two words from the list above.

_____

_____

_____

Unit 19
wh
ph
ch

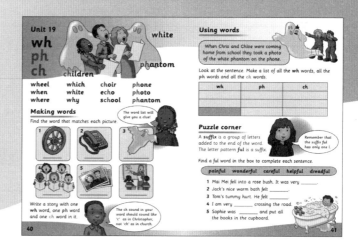

Targets
- to read and spell words containing the consonant digraphs *wh, ph, ch* (as in 'Christopher')
- to spell words with the common suffix *ful*

Word list

wheel	which	choir	phone
when	white	echo	photo
where	why	school	phantom

Some other relevant words

what

whale while

whisper whistle

whatever whenever

anywhere everywhere somewhere

meanwhile

phrase

graph photograph

dolphin elephant

Relevant high-frequency words

what when where school

Pupil Book answers
Making words

1 wheel **2** phone **3** phantom

4 choir **5** photo **6** school

Child's own short story including at least one word with each of the target consonant digraphs.

Using words

Words used in the sentence:

wh: when white

ph: photo phantom phone

ch: Chris Chloe school

Puzzle corner

1 painful **2** wonderful **3** dreadful

4 careful **5** helpful

Copymaster/Homework answers
Unit 19A

dolphin whistle echo school

A *funny* sentence or two using the words: elephant whisper Chloe.

Unit 19B

Write the **ful** word with the picture – mouthful dreadful beautiful handful painful helpful.

Suggestions

- Before starting work with this unit, revise Book 1, Unit 7 and Book 2, Unit 11, in which the *ch* digraph has its more common phoneme (as in 'chat'). In the context of this unit the *h* is effectively 'silent'.

- The *wh* digraph has a different pronunciation in different dialects, so appropriate adaption of activities should be made. In most areas the *h* can be taught as a silent letter, but not in all parts of the UK, notably Scotland.

- The *ph* digraph has come down to our language from Greek. This gives an early opportunity to introduce children to the notion of English being derived from several other languages. Here are some examples: phone – voice or sound; graph – writing; sphere – ball; photo – light.

- Select carefully the root words being introduced to minimise complications that might arise from adding the target suffix. Discuss the notion of root words, showing the children that when *ful* is added a new but related word is created.

- Ensure the children are clear that when *ful* is used as a suffix it has a single *l*, rather than *ll* (as in the word 'full').

Name: _____ Date: _____

Match the word to the picture.

> **whistle   echo   school   dolphin**

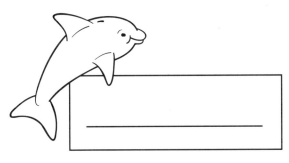

Colour the pictures.

Write a sentence or two using the words in the box.

> **elephant   whisper   Chloe**

_____

_____

_____

_____

Unit 19B

Write the word to match the picture.

> **painful beautiful mouthful**
> **handful helpful dreadful**

_____

_____

_____

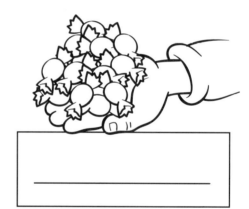

_____

_____

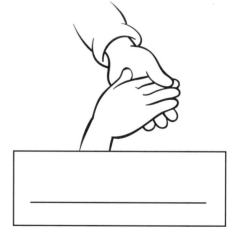

_____

Colour the picture you like best.

Unit 20
wa

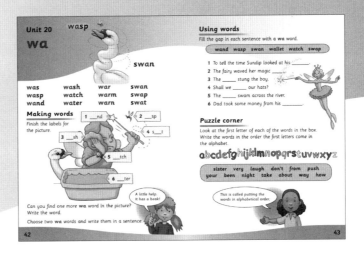

Targets
- to practise the letter pattern *wa*
- to read on sight and spell high-frequency words

Word list

was	wash	war	swan
wasp	watch	warm	swap
wand	water	warn	swat

Some other relevant words

wallet want ward
swamp

Relevant high-frequency words

water want

Pupil Book answers
Making words

1 wand **2** wasp **3** wash **4** swat
5 watch **6** water
extra word: swan
Child's own sentence incorporating two **wa** words.

Using words

1 watch **2** wand **3** wasp **4** swap
5 swan **6** wallet

Puzzle corner

The alphabetical order is:
about been don't from how laugh night
push sister take very way your.

Copymaster/Homework answers
Unit 20A
Child's own six **wa** words and completed
wordsearch.
Unit 20B
High-frequency words – after school home
another back these with pull
Other words that can be made by joining the letters
– hose ball bath base wick will wise puck

Suggestions
- Four of the most frequent irregular words (water, want, was, wasn't) include this spelling pattern.
- Copymaster 20B can be adjusted for difficulty by the teacher completing some of the connections before the child commences work, thus eliminating some of the options.

Make your own wordsearch for family and friends.

Unit 20A

Write six words with the letters **wa**.

_____	_____	_____
_____	_____	_____

Now make your wordsearch.

Put the **wa** words you have chosen in the grid first, then fill in the gaps with other letters.

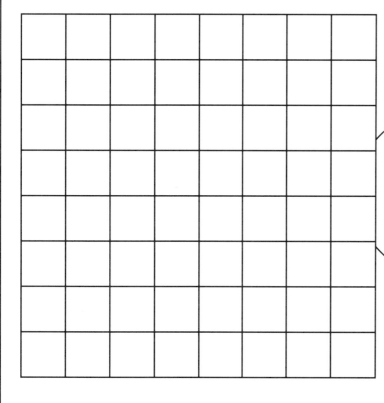

When someone tries your wordsearch remember to cover the six **wa** words above. These are the answers!

Name: _____   Date: _____

Make a word.

Match the letters by drawing a line between them.
Write the word. The first one is done for you.

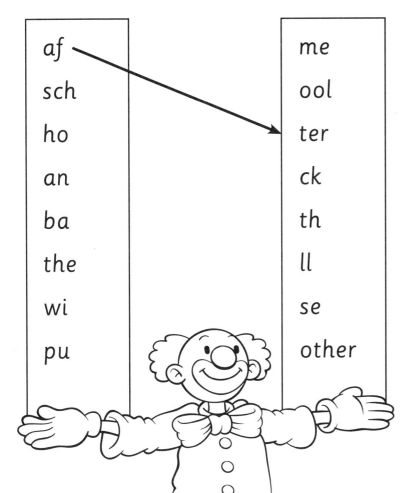

af	me
sch	ool
ho	ter
an	ck
ba	th
the	ll
wi	se
pu	other

_____

_____

after _____

_____

_____

_____

_____

_____

Write any more words you can make by joining
the letters above.

_____

_____

_____

Unit 21
ear

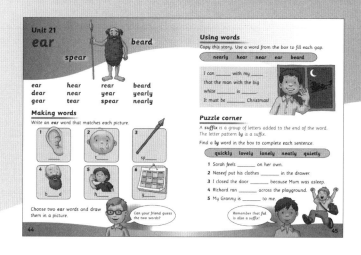

Targets

- to discriminate, spell and read the most common spelling pattern for the vowel phoneme *ear*
- to spell words with the common suffix *ly*

Word list

ear	hear	rear	beard
dear	near	year	yearly
gear	tear	spear	nearly

Some other relevant words

fear

clear smear

dearly

Relevant high-frequency words

No relevant words.

Pupil Book answers

Making words

1 ear **2** tear **3** spear **4** beard

5 hear **6** year

An illustration incorporating two **ear** words.

Using words

The **ear** words used in the story are (in order):
hear ear beard near nearly.

Puzzle corner

1 lonely **2** neatly **3** quietly

4 quickly **5** lovely

Copymaster/Homework answers

Unit 21A

nearly year beard hear ear tear

A sentence that includes an **ear** word, together with a picture.

Unit 21B

friendly lonely quickly extremely lovely quietly

A sentence using one of these words.

Suggestions

- This unit focuses on the *ear* grapheme, by far the most common representation of the target phoneme. With those children who are ready the teacher might introduce other spelling patterns for the phoneme, e.g. *ere* (here), *eer* (beer).

- Make a class collection of *ear* words, and a parallel collection of words with other words representing the same phoneme. It can be fun to write the collected words on outlines of ears and from these create a mobile.

- As with the *ful* suffix, practised in Unit 19, select carefully the root words being introduced to minimise complications that might arise from adding the target suffix. Before undertaking Copymaster 21B, discuss the notion of root words, showing the children that when *ly* is removed from each of the activity words, a 'root' word is left. Then, move on to inviting children to add back the *ly* suffix to each word. In oral exercises, put the root word and the root+suffix word into sentences.

Name: _____   Date: _____

Finish the sentences with the **ear** words.

| tear   nearly   beard   ear   year   hear |

I _____ slipped over on the ice!

Next _____ I will be seven years old.

Father Christmas has a big white _____.

Tuhil could _____ the music through his _____.

Sarah was upset. She had a _____ on her cheek.

Write your own sentence using an **ear** word.

_____

_____

_____

Draw a picture of it.

Choose a word with a **ly** suffix
to complete each sentence.

> quietly   lonely   lovely
> quickly   extremely   friendly

I like Jermaine. He is very _____ to me.

I feel _____ without my friends.

I got dressed _____ as I was
late for school.

I forgot my umbrella.
I got _____ wet!

The sun is shining.
What a _____ day.

We must talk _____ in the library.

Write a sentence using one of the above **ly** words.

_____

_____

_____

Unit 22
ea

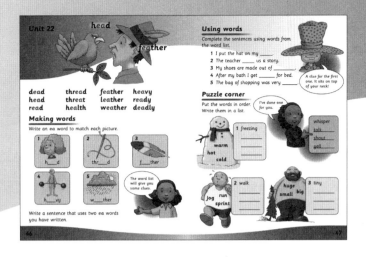

Targets

- to discriminate, spell and read the common spelling pattern for the vowel phoneme *ea* (as in 'bread')
- to collect and discuss similarities and shades of meaning

Word list

dead	thread	feather	heavy
head	threat	leather	ready
read	health	weather	deadly

Some other relevant words

deaf lead

bread dread stead

heaven

meadow

tread treasure

spread

already steady

weapon

dreadful breakfast jealous

Relevant high-frequency words

No relevant words.

Pupil Book answers

Making words

1 head **2** thread **3** feather

4 heavy **5** weather

A sentence including two **ea** words.

Using words

1 head **2** read **3** leather

4 ready **5** heavy

Puzzle corner

Shades of meaning written in this order:

1 freezing cold warm hot

2 walk jog run sprint

3 tiny small big huge

Copymaster/Homework answers

Unit 21A

Add the **ea** words to the picture:

bread meadow treasure breakfast head.

Write a sentence about the picture.

Unit 21B

drink – sip swallow gulp

big – huge enormous great

sleepy – drowsy tired asleep

Child's own word added to each beehive.

Suggestions

- As with the phoneme represented by *ear* (Unit 21), make a class collection of words, separating them into two lists dependent on the phoneme, i.e. *ea* as in 'head', *ea* as in 'bead'. Arrange the words on appropriate visual prompts, such as loaves of bread and on large beads hung on a string.

- Make sets of flashcards which selected children hold up in front of the class or group. Other children suggest the order in which the children holding the cards should stand to grade the meanings of the words – as demonstrated in the *Puzzle corner* and Copymaster 22B.

Unit 22A

Add the **ea** words to the picture.

| bread   meadow   treasure   breakfast   head |

Write a sentence about the picture.

_____

_____

_____

_____

Unit 22B

Join the similar words to the
correct beehive. Write the words in the beehive.
The first word is done for you.

asleep

swallow

great

big

tired

huge

gulp

Can you add
one more word
to each beehive?

sip

enormous

drowsy

sleepy

drink

Pupil Assessments

Assessment notes and answers
Book 2 Pupil Assessment A
Book 2 Pupil Assessment B

Assessment notes and answers

Notes

- There are two assessments: Pupil Assessment A covering Units 1–11 and Pupil Assessment B covering Units 12–22 from the *Pupil Book*.

- Each question represents the spelling focus of a unit.

- The questions the pupil struggles with represent the spelling focus the child needs further work on.

- It is suggested the child does the assessment in a relatively quiet environment.

Answers

Pupil Assessment A

1   sea   tree   sheep   steam
2   hay   face   nail   snake
3   kite   fly   light (or light bulb)
4   Pupil selects two words to rhyme with **float**, e.g. goat   boat
5   moon   glue   blue   crew   June
6   Pupil selects two words that rhyme with **back**, e.g. lack   crack   jack
7   bull   wood   hood   hook
8   car   arm   shark   barge (or boat)
9   Pupil selects two words that end in **joy**, e.g. boy   toy
10   mouth   cow
11   witch   punch

Pupil Assessment B

1   stairs
2   bear   hare
3   cork   fork   horn   core
4   Pupil selects a words that rhymes with: dawn, e.g. lawn   straw, e.g. raw
5   winter   letter
6   Pupil draws picture to illustrate a chosen **ir** word.
7   Pupil selects two words that rhyme with **churn**, e.g. burn   turn
8   when   school   photo   white   choir   phone
9   wasp   watch   swan   wash
10   Child selects three words that end in **ear**.
11   Pupil selects a words that rhymes with: feather, e.g. leather   dead, e.g. head   dread, e.g. bread

Name: _____ Date: _____

1 Finish each word
to match the pictures.

| s____ | tr____ | sh___p | st___m |

2 Finish each word to match the pictures.

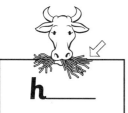  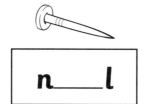 

| h____ | f__c__ | n___l | sn__k__ |

3 Write a word to match each picture.

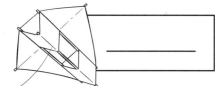 _____   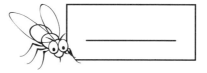 _____    _____

4 Write two words with the same spelling pattern
and that rhyme with **float**.

| _____ | _____ |

5 Write a word to answer each puzzle.

Seen in the sky at night – but not stars.   m_____

Something that sticks things together.   g_____

A colour than rhymes with **true**.   b_____

People who work on a boat.   c_____

Name: _____   Date: _____

The sixth month.  J_____

6 Write two words that have the same spelling pattern and rhyme with **back**.

_____   _____

7 Write a word to match each picture.

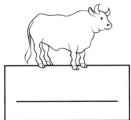 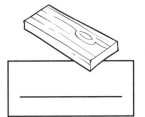 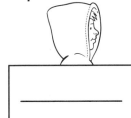 

_____   _____   _____   _____

8 Finish these words.

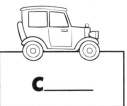   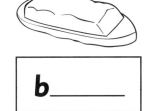

c____   ____m   sh_____   b_____

9 Write two words that end in **oy**.

_____   _____

10 Add **ow** or **ou** to match the word with the picture.

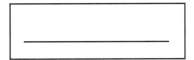 m____th   c____

11 Write a word that matches each picture.

_____ 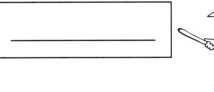   _____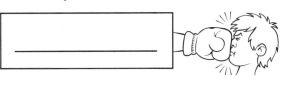

Name: _____   Date: _____

1 You often climb these to go to bed.

2 Write an **ear** or **are** word to match each picture.

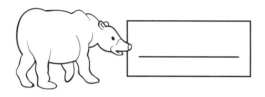   

3 Write a word to answer each puzzle.

This fits in the top of a bottle.   c_____

Something used to eat with a knife.   **f**_____

A rhino has one on his nose.   **h**_____

The centre of an apple.   **c**_____

4 Write a word that has the same spelling pattern and rhymes with each of these words.

dawn _____   straw _____

5 Find a word that ends with **er** to answer the clues.

The season after autumn.   _____

The postman brought me one.   _____

Name: _____   Date: _____

6 Draw a picture of an **ir** word. Write the word.

_____

7 Write two words that have the same spelling pattern and rhyme with **churn**.

_____   _____

8 Add **wh**, **ph** or **ch** to finish these words.

| __ __en | s__ __ool | __ __oto | __ __ite |

| __ __oir | __ __one |

9 Finish each word to match the pictures.

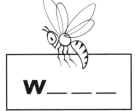 **w**____    **w**_____    **s**____    **w**____

10 Write three words that end in **ear**.

_____   _____   _____

11 Write a rhyming word with the same spelling pattern.

feather _____   dead _____

dread _____

Look Cover Say Write Check

Unit word lists

High-frequency (HF) word lists

Look Cover Say Write Check copymaster

Look Cover Say Write Check

Unit word lists

The following lists of words from each unit are designed to be photocopied. If required they can be stuck to the photocopiable sheet on page 96 and used as the spelling homework for the week. The words can be split according to the ability of the child, e.g. one child might take home all twelve spellings while another may take just six.

High-frequency words

It is important that the children are very familiar with the high-frequency words. It is crucial they learn to spell them as soon as they are able. As well as having various exercises throughout the scheme we have also included them as lists of spelling/homework words. The words have been listed in groups of six, as logically as possible.

We haven't included in the list colour, month, day and number words as classrooms tend to cover these thoroughly. However, they can be found in exercises throughout the *Pupil Books*.

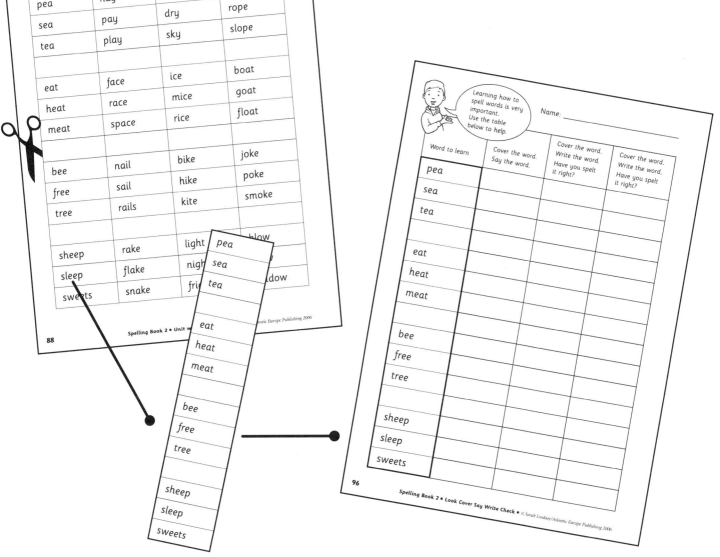

Unit word lists

Unit 1	Unit 2	Unit 3	Unit 4
pea	hay	cry	hope
sea	pay	dry	rope
tea	play	sky	slope
eat	face	ice	boat
heat	race	mice	goat
meat	space	rice	float
bee	nail	bike	joke
free	sail	hike	poke
tree	rails	kite	smoke
sheep	rake	light	blow
sleep	flake	night	snow
sweets	snake	fright	window

Unit word lists

Unit 5	Unit 6	Unit 7	Unit 8
few	back	bull	ark
new	rack	full	arm
chew	sack	pull	art
blue	deck	book	bar
clue	neck	cook	barn
true	peck	hook	barge
June	kick	good	car
tune	lick	hood	jar
prune	tick	wood	star
moon	duck	brook	bark
spoon	muck	shook	dark
balloon	clock	stood	shark

Unit word lists

Unit 9	Unit 10	Unit 11	Unit 12
boy	cow	catch	air
joy	how	match	fair
toy	now	patch	hair
oil	owl	itch	pair
boil	howl	witch	flair
soil	growl	stitch	stair
join	out	finch	hairs
joint	about	pinch	pairs
point	shout	bunch	stairs
noise	couch	lunch	chair
voice	pouch	munch	funfair
choice	slouch	punch	airport

Unit word lists

Unit 13	Unit 14	Unit 15	Unit 16
care	cork	jaw	her
hare	fork	paw	herd
rare	pork	saw	ever
bear	born	dawn	after
pear	corn	lawn	clever
tear	horn	yawn	corner
scare	bore	claw	letter
share	core	draw	water
spare	more	straw	winter
swear	sore	cause	computer
wear	tore	pause	newspaper
wearing	wore	because	September

Unit word lists

Unit 17	Unit 18	Unit 19	Unit 20
fir	burn	wheel	was
sir	turn	when	wasp
stir	churn	where	wand
bird	fur	which	wash
firm	curl	white	watch
third	hurl	why	water
dirt	hurt	choir	war
shirt	surf	echo	warm
skirt	turf	school	warn
birth	curse	phone	swan
first	nurse	photo	swap
thirst	purse	phantom	swat

 Spelling Book 2 • Unit word lists • © *Sarah Lindsay/Atlantic Europe Publishing 2006*

Unit word lists/High-frequency (HF) word lists

Unit 21	Unit 22	HF 1	HF 3
ear	dead	an	did
dear	head	as	dig
gear	read	had	his
		has	if
hear	thread	man	will
near	threat	ran	with
tear	health		
		HF 2	**HF 4**
rear	feather	bed	but
year	leather	red	jump
spear	weather	help	just
		next	must
beard	heavy	got	much
yearly	ready	not	us
nearly	deadly		

High-frequency (HF) word lists

HF 5	HF 7	HF 9	HF 11
ball	another	again	home
call	brother	came	over
will	been	name	good
pull	seen	made	new
push	three	make	there
should	tree	take	too
HF 6	**HF 8**	**HF 10**	**HF 12**
than	first	may	back
that	just	way	put
their	last	time	pull
them	must	live	took
then	sister	by	boy
these	our	night	from

High-frequency (HF) word lists

HF 13	HF 15	HF 17	HF 19
now	what	would	people
down	when	could	little
how	where	do	laugh
out	school	don't	love
about	first	can't	many
house	girl	some	your
HF 14	**HF 16**	**HF 18**	**HF 20**
water	door	be	half
after	more	here	have
her	or	him	old
over	saw	so	once
one	because	off	very
two	want	who	were

Learning how to spell words is very important.
Use the table below to help.

Name: _____

Word to learn	Cover the word. Say the word.	Cover the word. Write the word. Have you spelt it right?	Cover the word. Write the word. Have you spelt it right?

 Spelling Book 2 • **Look Cover Say Write Check** • © *Sarah Lindsay/Atlantic Europe Publishing 2006*